FinTech

Financial Technology and Modern Finance in the 21st Century

By Jeff Reed

© **Copyright 2016 by Jeff Reed. All rights reserved.**

This document is geared towards providing exact and reliable information in regards to the topic and issue covered. The publication is sold with the idea that the publisher is not required to render accounting, officially permitted, or otherwise, qualified services. If advice is necessary, legal or professional, a practiced individual in the profession should be ordered.

- From a Declaration of Principles which was accepted and approved equally by a Committee of the American Bar Association and a Committee of Publishers and Associations.

In no way is it legal to reproduce, duplicate, or transmit any part of this document in either electronic means or in printed format. Recording of this publication is strictly prohibited and any storage of this document is not allowed unless with written permission from the publisher. All rights reserved.

The information provided herein is stated to be truthful and consistent, in that any liability, in terms of inattention or otherwise, by any usage or abuse of any policies, processes, or directions contained within is the solitary and utter responsibility of the recipient reader. Under no circumstances will any legal responsibility or blame be held against the publisher for any reparation, damages, or monetary loss due to the information herein, either directly or indirectly.

Respective authors own all copyrights not held by the publisher.

The information herein is offered for informational purposes solely, and is universal as so. The presentation of the information is without contract or any type of guarantee assurance.

The trademarks that are used are without any consent, and the publication of the trademark is without permission or backing by the trademark owner. All trademarks and brands within this book are for clarifying purposes only and are the owned by the owners themselves, not affiliated with this document.

Table of Contents

Introduction 1

Chapter 1: New Realities 3

Chapter 2: Fintech's Impact on a Global Economy 17

Chapter 3: The "End User" Experience 19

Chapter 4: The Payment Ecosystem 33

Chapter 5: FinTech and the B2B Sector 43

Chapter 6: FinTech and Investing 50

Chapter 7: Fintech and Online Banking 58

Chapter 8: A Peek into the Future 63

Other Publications 70

Introduction

FinTech simply means financial technology. Companies such as Apple and Facebook have both taken the lead in developing these technologies - you can send money directly through applications with both of these entities. The start-up mentality is no longer limited to the tech industry; it is revolutionizing finance as well.

Chapter 1

New Realities

Investment in financial technology is booming at unprecedented rates. Despite traditional banking protests, the world of banking is going through a transformation and will continue to go through a change. Take a look at how things were done ten years ago, now think about how they will be done ten years down the road. With all the new technology that we have today, it is almost mind-blowing to think about the kind of technology that we will have in another ten years or so. The change is going to keep coming, the only thing we can do is get on board with it.

FinTech

When the twenty-first century came around, a new financial service emerged, and it was known as financial technology or FinTech. This term originally was used to describe the technology that was used by consumers and trades done by financial institutions. However, at the end of the first decade, of the twenty-first century, it now includes any technological innovation that has been made within the financial sector. This includes any innovations that have been made in education, retail banking, financial literacy, and even cryptocurrencies.

Several companies have used or are getting into the FinTech movement in order to make things easier on their customers. These companies are constantly evolving in how they accept payments, send payments, and handle their client's money in general.

PayPal

In the 1990s, PayPal began to change the face of traditional banking through the use of financial technology. Even today, they continue to be a leader in the FinTech movement. They are also steadily growing as the prime choice for payment for many online and even retail businesses outside of the consumer using cash or a credit card.

There has been an enormous growth in the payment process that was acquired by PayPal called Braintree. Within the first two years, Braintree was able to announce that the payment volume that was authorized was about fifty billion. However, the stock continued to trade flat in July.

Despite this, PayPal still remains to be one of the largest sites that chosen when it comes to online transfers of money, whether it be for friends and family, for paychecks, or even goods and services that have been purchased. This makes it a vital part of FinTech.

Apple Pay

Similar to PayPal, Apple Pay is a way that you can electronically transfer money from your bank account to either purchase something, or simply to act as a digital wallet. Apple Pay is only compatible with the newer versions of Apple's products.

One of the things that make Apple Pay unique is that it can work with any contactless terminals that already exist. Along with Apple Pay, there is the Apple Watch which is known as "your wallet without the wallet." With Apple Watch, you are able to use Apple Pay in a variety of different retailers.

Being that Apple is providing a financial service that is making a difference in the economy, it makes Apple Pay part of the FinTech movement. Apple has also paired with some of the top FinTech investors such as Stripe in order to contribute to making a further impact. Thanks to all of the service that Apple Pay has done for their customers, it is exciting to watch and see what Apple is planning to do with their financial services next.

What Lies Ahead

When first looking at FinTech, there has been an increase of $12.21 billion in investments since 2014. However, there are some complications with FinTech as there is with anything. But, despite the fact that there are complications, it is believed that the financial services that are already established are going to continue to not only survive, but thrive because they are going to find ways to grow during the digital future. Some people believe the financial institutes that are already established are not going to survive because of FinTech and are going to die off due to a loss of market shares.

Two scenarios can shed some light on the structure for what can possibly happen. It is important to know that these scenarios are going to apply to all banks because all banks still have the ability to control their own destiny.

Scenario one: with all the new changes, the banks end up being lost to the new financial services that are more efficient and in touch with the digital world that we live in. Although the bank will continue their product based sales in order to get customers instead of trying to improve their customer experience.

The banks that are in this scenario are going to be competing because their brands are going to fall on the eyes of their customers to nothing more than a utility that they can use. But, they will continue to think that their business model and strategies will remain the most successful.

Scenario two: unlike scenario one, banks focus on making the customer's life easier and accept changes to the business model instead of sticking to the old ways. While the customers tell the banks what they want to see, they are helping to shape the bank's way of business which will delight their customers.

Unless banks adapt to the digital era, banks are going to have only a short-term advantage because they will not be solving problems that frustrate their customers. In the end, banks can either conform to the digital age and make sure that they are addressing what frustrates their customers. Or, they can end up losing customers and potentially risk being obsolete because they will cease being convenient for the client.

Peer to Peer (P2P)

Peer to Peer lending was meant to help make things easier when it comes to doing business. When seeking money, you are not going to be getting the money from a bank loan. Instead, you will be getting it from other small businesses. Not only that, but some platforms accurately match lenders to borrowers. This is where the entire industry emerges; theses platforms cut costs by serving as intermediaries.

The history of peer to peer lending is short. The first company to emerge began in 2005, with Zopa, in the UK. The first serious large-scale operation launched in 2010 to allow for peer to business lending.

There have been setbacks in the development; with so much innovation, some models do not always succeed. One company closed down with 100% defaults because it's model of operation did not encourage people to pay each other back. Thus caution must be exercised.

Below, is a list of the defining characteristics of peer to peer practices:

- Peer to peer lending takes place with the ultimate goal of profit in mind
- Lenders and borrowers are not matched up based on previous experiences with one another; often, they are total strangers. This means that unlike business to business practices of the past, there is not necessarily a lot of networking going on.
- The borrowing is facilitated through a third party company.

- Trading occurs online.
- Depending on the format of the company facilitating the lending, borrowers choose whom they are giving their money to directly.
- The money in the transaction is not necessarily secured; this also means there is little governmental intervention or regulation. Without security, there is some risk to be encountered, but in the UK there are funds established that are meant to protect those involved offered by a select few companies.
- The money being lent operates as securities which are capable of being transferred to other lenders or borrowers, to compensate for other costs incurred in the transaction process. Whether or not this is a possibility depends on entirely upon the platform being used. It is also not necessarily a free transaction and can, in fact, be comparatively costly.

In the early days of peer to peer lending, these companies often relied on social media as a way of facilitating transactions, but as development takes its hold, this is becoming more and more seldom. What makes P2P particularly potent is that unlike traditional intermediary structures, P2P relies on the community's implicit trust; all are in it together. With this democratic form of functioning, people seem to operate with more accountability. People are generally seen as acting with a sense of responsibility toward one another that is hard to imitate in traditional banking; simply put people don't have sympathy for the banking institutions as they do to other people. Despite the popularity among some groups of direct transactions, such as through the Bitcoin Blockchain, there is still a lot to be said for the emergence of the financial intermediaries. One benefit of these platforms is that they open up investment opportunities and provide exposure to companies that otherwise would have never had the chance to come into contact with one another.

P2P lending companies typically encompass the following services:

- Platform online that allows borrowers to solicit lenders and/or investors with a specific tailoring to their financial needs as defined by specific criteria.
- Applications to develop credit models which accurately determine approvals, costs, and appropriate pricing.
- The ability to verify borrower identity by checking out the accuracy of information supplied by their bank, employment, etc.
- Assessing the qualifications of borrowers to determine whether they are legitimate and regularly performing credit checks.
- Handling the payments from borrowers to lenders.
- Loan collection and customer service for all parties involved.
- Dealing with legal paperwork and reporting.

- Marketing the involvement of new lenders and borrowers to continually expand the market.

P2P networks earn their money by charging a one-time fee to all parties involved in return for the services they offer. These companies operate with very low overhead costs compared to banks because they exist entirely online, unlike banks. Because of this, the products and services they offer come at a lower cost. Another prime advantage of P2P is that they often operate with far lower interest rates.

Bitcoin and Other FinTech Startups

In order to understand the block chain model and how it is going to be transformative, it is important to understand how block chain works. Blockchain works off of a system of checks. The nodes monitor the transactions that are done within the system and then once they have been validated, they are added to the chain.

Essentially, blockchain can cut out the middle man and still maintain the liability that is provided by the teams of analysts and financial firms. Not only does it cut out the middle man, but it saves companies on the cost of labor. Along with that, it decreases the time that is needed for paperwork to be completed in order to have a transaction validated. The reduced time makes customers happy and makes things flow smoothly.

Bitcoin allows users to mine and earn bitcoins that can be spent within the server and are slowly becoming an acceptable currency with retailers.

While some of the more well-known FinTech products have been discussed, there are several that are not as well known, and use financial technology in order to keep customers happy when it comes to financial services that they can use.

Square: while this is known to some people, it is not known to everyone. This platform allows many retail stores along with restaurants that may not be largely known to accept credit card payments by using Android or iOS. Along with accepting credit cards, this tool tracks inventory and offers invoicing as well as real-time analytics. There are also customer engagement tools that are provided through this service.

As of August 2015, Square proudly announced that they had made an app that was compatible with Apple Watch so that their users were allowed to make P2P payments.

Mentioned earlier, Braintree began in 2007 and processes around four billion dollars in credit card volume annually from thousands of different retailers with about a billion being focused on mobile payments. Braintree has given the support that a lot of high-growth companies need. Companies such as LivingSocial, Uber, and even GitHub. PayPal eventually purchased Braintree in 2013.

Chapter 2

Fintech's Impact on a Global Economy

The disruptive power of financial technology is nowhere more apparent than in the realm of global finance. This is both a good and bad thing. It is good because there is considerable potential for development here, but it also poses an inherent risk to many jobs. In fact, one report by Citigroup estimated almost 30% of employees in the global financial sector are in danger of having their jobs eliminated by FinTech. Why is that? Well, financial technology is about interconnectivity. As such, it is easy to imagine that many jobs which are based solely on facilitated communication between various global markets that just do not need to exist. These jobs can be easily overtaken by technology that is, not only more accurate but also much quicker than having humans communicate with one another.

FinTech offers accessibility, to everyone with a reliable internet connection - no significant infrastructure necessary. In a rare turn of global events, it is not the banks of the US and North America who are dominating the development in this sector. China has embraced investment into these technologies at even higher levels. Banks in Africa and South East Asia are well aware of the potential for making lucrative profits in these markets. They are uncharted territory and fair game for everyone.

Chapter 3

The "End User" Experience

Part of what distinguishes FinTech and makes it particularly disruptive to the finance industry is that it is geared toward the customer's experience. Unlike banks, which have been able to function irrespective of the needs of its customers for decades, FinTech is required to be user-friendly in order to attract participants. No one needs to be convinced to open an account with a bank - but you do need convincing to try out something radically new and different such as online lending. The best way to attract users is to make it worth their while and user-friendly. Banks often develop online tools, but they are far from easy in terms of operability. Most do not design with customer needs in mind. That's where FinTech comes in and changes the market.

The user experience is the one thing that distinguishes your product from everyone else's. Besides that, people will not want to use your product if the experience is not user-friendly. What is to stop someone from using cash if they see that using technology is actually more of a hassle than pulling out their real wallet? Well, Fintech outperforms real banks because the competition is so much higher for customers, so their performance exceeds expectations.

What Makes User Experience Successful?

Successful end user experience is not only functional but attractive. This requires a whole new understanding of banking technologies. Since when has finance ever strove to be visually appealing? A new generation of people involved with finance is needed to engineer successful end-user experience and, instead of MBAs, are armed with graphic design degrees.

The problem with most banks is that the apps they have associated with their services still conceive of online banking as an added service and fail to realize that online banking should actually be at the core of their customer's engagement with their services. The days of the physical bank branches are slowly becoming a thing of the past.

The success of apps such as Venmo provides a solid template of how to understand user oriented financial services. The idea behind a good design essentially stipulates that the user should not realize they are using a financial service at all.

Guidelines to Live By

One of the troubles with FinTech is that the app needs to function in a way that verifies the identity of the operator. Otherwise, how can people trust in the veracity of the service they are operating if they cannot be sure they are exchanging money with legitimate individuals who have solid credit backgrounds? This principle is called Know your customer. The problem with the Know Your Customer approach is that it takes a lot of effort to correctly determine a person's identity electronically.

Here are some tips for simplifying the overwhelming task of getting to know your customers.

- Don't ask for all the information at once. This is time-consuming, and people will be suspicious of your service if you go for it all at once. The best way to collect customer information is to start with the bare minimum, then allows them to complete the first transaction. After trust in your service has been established, you are free to get the rest of the necessary info.

- Make it easy. Of course, you could ask your customers to scan and upload physical copies of their identifying documents, but that is a huge hassle for them. Partnering with other identity servicing companies to gather this information reduces the burden on your customers. Using the information, they have provided; these services will attempt to match photos from their database. In the event that this fails to work out, you can always ask then for a scan

- Give them reasons. People are naturally skeptical about offering up personal information, especially when it seems hard to understand what your gender could possibly have to do with their finances. This is why it is best to always explain why you are asking for certain information. These exchanges have to be based on trust, and the best practice for establishing trust is transparency.

- But don't make it too easy. Even Venmo has come under fire for their security failures. These technologies have to be simple to interact with, but not so simple that they can be easily hacked. Customers have to feel safe using your app, which is why simple features such a security pins are essential. This is where FinTech user experience differs from the user experience of other applications. Unlike photo sharing apps, messaging, etc., there is an element of security in the design that must be present which is not required for other platforms.

User Experience Guidelines

Every company wants to have a user experience that brings a quality experience to their users. However, it is harder for the business to create the ultimate user experience in financial services. When working with finances, it is important to have a high level of security on the data that you are given by your customer along with protecting their assets. As a financial institute, you are going to want to provide an experience that is friendly but provides the level of security that your customers are expecting. The only way to do this is to follow a set of guidelines that will provide the customer service that you are seeking.

Consider your user's experience: it is a common mistake that many companies learn from. If you think about your customer's experience from the beginning, then you are going to be able to provide the experience that they expect and deserve. FinTech is still relatively new, which causes some consumers to be leery of it. But, you can ease their fears by offering them answers to their questions and the support that they need in order to have a good experience. Keep in mind, what would you like to experience when you go to your financial institute? If you would not like the service that you are providing your customers, then why are you providing it to them?

People are afraid of money: many people are afraid to know the truth about money. The amount of money that we earn is finite, and some day it will stop being made. While there are other ways that money can come into a customer's life, such as the lottery, it is unlikely that it will be won by your client. The average American often dreams of having a lot of money but has no grasp on the basics of finances. Debt and negative account balances often times place a shadow over their financial future. But, you are able to help with this by providing them with the resources that they need in order to turn their financial future around.

Customers have a financial lifespan: every customer is going to change how their view their finances based on where they are in their life. The products that you are offering should tie in closely to where they are in their life so that you are appealing to the customer across their financial lifetime.

Complexity will never disappear: the user's experience is only going to be as good as the products that are offered, but no union will be absolutely perfect between the two, though. There are going to be parts of FinTech that involve regulations as well as legal "badlands." With this knowledge, you are still going to be able to determine the complexity that is not necessary so that you can eliminate noise that is caused due to the laws that you are going to have to comply with. The best that you can do is to try and listen to your customers and advocate for sensible changes.

Find the pain, and remove it: there was a poll that was conducted by the Times for people who are between the ages of twenty-three and thirty-three that have said they would rather deal with dental procedures over dealing with a banker. But, there is no pain if you want gains. So, this is where the financial institute needs to step back and determine what pain is being caused by red tape and what pain is because caused by things that can be changed. Clear up any unnecessary confusion, bureaucratic hurdles, and increasing reliability. Make changes that are going to allow your user to feel secure while understanding their financial lives.

Engineering and design: when creating an application or website that a customer is going to interact with, the lines of code need to work as they were intended to work. This is going to play a significant role in how the customer experience plays out because a client is going to deal with the technological side of banking before they deal with an actual person. This is just because it is easier to check their account when they are sitting in the pickup line at school rather than having to schedule time between everything else that is going on in their lives to come into the bank and wait in line to talk to someone. The quality of the code is going to be the core of any FinTech experience along with how a customer feels about that particular brand and how often they use that product.

Look at programs like Instagram. There are millions of users on it every day because the coding behind it is written so that the process of taking a picture and uploading it is seamless and does not require a long drawn out process to upload a picture.

The function of the application should blend in with the engineering of the application. The form should never be sacrificed for function because both are equally important to how the user experience.

Trust and simplicity: as mentioned above, there can be some pain involved when it comes to banking. But, it is important to establish trust with your customers. FinTech applications are not in a great spot as far as the public's opinion is concerned. This forces them to compete against established financial institutions when it comes to the various functions that they offer. Customers have certain expectations when it comes to the applications that they use, and the thought behind the design of an application ultimately needs to be the client's experience when they are using it. The experience should be a positive one for the customer.

Reliability needs to be perceived at a higher rate along with the level of data importance when it comes to the consumer applications. If reliability and data importance are not at the top of the list when it comes to the design, then that application is not going to be able to compete.

The security measures that are being taken should be clear because with FinTech, you are dealing with people's money and that is something that they take seriously. Money is how they are able to survive in a world that is becoming harder to survive in. Every last dollar counts to many families. When a user understands all the security measures that are being implemented, they are going to trust a little more because they know that their financial well-being is being looked after by someone else as well. FinTech applications should be designed so that there is a password recovery system that is easy to use. Not everyone is going to have access to the email that they started the account with, so offer them a variety of ways that they can recover their password. Do not make the recovery process overly demanding cause this can lead to a customer becoming frustrated and not completing the process.

Customization is important to customers. They want things to resemble the topics that are important to them. No two people are the same, so why should their application experience be the same? When designing an application, the consumer should be able to make it their own. This is going to make the customer feel more valued and more likely to continue using that brand.

Any new technology should be advanced, but not beyond its time. Once the security of a company has been established, then that company needs to appeal to the mainstream. No company is going to be able to stay afloat without customers; it is just a simple fact of how businesses work. But, the technology that is used by that company needs to be easy for people to understand and trust. In order to do this, make sure that your brand is frequently seen by customers so that they are likely to use it in the future.

The speed of decisions: no matter what application it is, FinTech is purely digital. Because of this, they can be iterated for a low cost in short order. The turnaround of FinTech applications is beneficial for a number of reasons. First, the application can be easily tuned based on the customer feedback that they receive. When something has to be physically changed, it takes up a lot of time and is unrealistic because the design team is going to have to modify the paradigms at a rate that may not be entirely possible for them to do.

When changes go live, a team has to act accordingly and hope that everything is as it should be. However, when it is digital, it is easy to update and thus ensuring any compliance to regulations is met to the fullest.

With everything being digital, the cost of changing things is significantly reduced more than the traditional way that things have been done. When an application is put together, it is a process that requires several people and is done in a matter of weeks now instead of months.

Chapter 4

The Payment Ecosystem

In a traditional financial ecosystem—based with credit cards or debit cards, there are four players: You have the cardholder or person making out the check, who gives the initial payment. Then, there is the merchant, who is the person getting the payment from the cardholder. John Smith is the cardholder, and the merchant is his local tailor. The issuer is an institution in charge of dealing with the services provided to the cardholder, such as providing him with a card, issuing bank statements, making sure his card isn't being stolen or identity mishandled. John Smith's issuer is, in other words, his bank. The acquirer is the equivalent of that entity for the merchant, so, the merchant's bank.

The transaction is pretty direct. John Smith's issue gave him a card, and he uses that card to make a purchase from his tailor. The information about this transaction is then exchanged from John Smith's bank to the bank of his tailor. Nowadays, all of this is done electronically. This model only works when there are only a few banks. As you are undoubtedly aware, this is definitely not the case. With so many banks, there had to be a way of organizing them. This method of organization which allows for a trusted intermediary to facilitate transactions between issuers and acquirers is called a scheme. Schemes you have heard of before are VISA and MasterCard. The role of the trusted intermediary is to give credibility to both parties involved in the financial transaction.

And, with the introduction of e-commerce into the ecosystem, things get a lot more complicated.

You may be thinking, what does an ecosystem have to do with financial technologies? The ecosystem is merely a word used to describe the way these technologies function and are interdependent upon each other, like the living things in an ecosystem are dependent upon one another. The payment ecosystem represents the way that all things get together in order to make a transaction possible.

Components of the Ecosystem

E-WALLETS

Otherwise known as mobile wallets, E-Wallets allow consumers to pay with a cell phone. E-Wallets are used to make electronic purchases via a smartphone and are facilitated by Near Field Communication (NFC). Consumers store credit card information in mobile wallets, creating a virtual credit card, and then pay by tapping the device on the terminal.

BANK CREDIT CARDS

These banks (issuers) issue credit cards on behalf of card brands. They provide consumers with credit cards, send credit card statements, and offer customers credit.

BUSINESS CREDIT CARDS

These are companies that can issue credit cards.

E-WALLET PLATFORMS

E-Wallet platforms are commerce infrastructures that businesses can configure to offer a mobile wallet solution.

CARD ASSOCIATIONS (CARD BRANDS)

Card associations are more commonly known as credit card and debit card companies. Their job is to govern compliance policies pertaining to their payment cards, monitor processing activity, develop new products, and oversee the clearing and settlement of transactions.

ACQUIRERS

Also known as an acquiring or merchant bank, acquirers take on the risk of credit card processing. They solicit, underwrite, and maintain the merchant account.

PROCESSORS

Payment processors are responsible for setting up the merchant account along with negotiating the rates for the setup, processing, and equipment that is needed. They act as a middleman between merchants and acquirers. They may also provide the technology and hardware which enables the merchant to process the transaction.

3rd Party Processors

Also known as aggregators, 3rd party processors allow merchants to accept payments without applying and acquiring a merchant account of their own.

INDEPENDENT SALES ORGANIZATION (ISO)

Also called a merchant service provider, an ISO is a third-party organization that is contracted by an acquirer and signs merchants up to accept credit cards.

POS TERMINAL TECHNOLOGY

The point of sale (POS) terminal technologies are the physical payment terminals that merchants accept in-store payments with.

INTEGRATED SYSTEMS

Integrated systems, or POS software, are what brick-and-mortar businesses use to conduct sales, run their business, and manage inventory. These systems can be operated on tablets, computers, and smartphones.

IN-STORE TERMINAL PROVIDERS

Traditional terminals are considered the most official payment channel. These providers equip merchants with hardware that allows them to swipe or insert the credit card to process the transaction.

E-COMMERCE PAYMENT PROCESSORS

From integrated APIs to hosted checkouts, e-commerce providers are enabling websites to simplify the checkout process and accept payments securely over the web. PayPal was one of the first companies to help businesses take credit cards online. These days, there are a lot more e-commerce players.

RECURRING BILLING PAYMENT PROCESSORS

Recurring billing payment processors allow merchants to automate payments on a scheduled basis for product or service subscriptions.

MOBILE PAYMENT PROCESSORS

Mobile payment processors allow merchants to accept payments using their existing mobile phones by keying the credit card number into an app or via an attached card swiper. This allows merchants to take payments wherever they are. Square first introduced the mobile swiper to the U.S. market, and Payfirma did the same for the Canadian market.

TABLET POS PROVIDERS

For small brick-and-mortar businesses, tablet POS are great as it removes the need for a bulky traditional register. Tablet POS providers enable merchants to run a full register using just a tablet and optional card swiper.

CLOSED LOOP PAYMENT NETWORKS

Closed loop payment processing is limited to a particular vendor or location. Consumers are able to load money into a spending account that is linked to a payment item (i.e. gift card for a specific company or a mobile app).

Wearable Technology and FinTech

Wearable technology, such as Apple Watches, are a critical part of the ecosystem that is not developed enough to be taken over by the new technology. They are a prime example of user experience.

Near Field Communication

Near field communications or NFC technologies occur when two electronic devices communicate as a direct result of their proximity to one another. In FinTech, this usually describes the technology in which a transaction is carried out in the presence of a secure element within a device that is connected to a payment organ. Apple Pay is an example of this. To envision this, think of the way Apple Pay works. The secure element exists in the smartphone. By bringing it close enough to the communicating device within the register, known as the point of sale terminal, the payment service is able to access the balance and carry out the transaction.

The limitations of NFC are somewhat apparent in that they are generally limited to in-store sales or when it comes to transportation services such as Uber or Lyft. Unlike much of FinTech, which is about the way these technologies can be used globally, NFC is inherently localized. This does have implications for a global economy, however, and could be utilized in place of the time-consuming process of currency exchanges. One service that requires consideration is the services that are blowing up in countries within Africa where many people do not own credit cards. This enables non-physical payment without the need for a bank account. There are still hurdles in the way of further developing these technologies.

Chapter 5

FinTech and the B2B Sector

B2B, or business to business, transactions refer to the relationships that businesses establish to make transactions with other business. An example of this is when one company buys raw materials from another one in order to make their product. This stands in contrast to business to consumer or business to government transactions. So what does B2B have to do with FinTech and the world of e-commerce?

Thanks to internet communication it is far simpler for businesses to come in contact with one another. Just the existence of a company website alone is enough to radically change the way businesses interact with one another. Through social media and other networking technologies, it is easier than ever to establish these often global connections.

Think of how Amazon functions, setting up individual vendors with buyers from around the world. Businesses can find out about products another company offers, and there are new technologies, such as directories, that are established in order to facilitate this process. These types of interactions no longer require face-to-face negotiations - it is as easy for B2B connections to be created online for consumers to order their products through the company's website.

Companies that offer B2B services have not historically been sites of innovation and capital flow - until now. With the advent of financial technologies, there has been a boom in the investments establishing B2B financial services. This has tremendous importance for anyone running a business or for developers.

These can take the form of mobile accounting apps to keep track of taxes or using cloud technology to make invoicing easier. Another area of innovation: security and anti-theft technologies to protect businesses and corporations. One company is working to make a program that offers online meal vouchers for its employees.

B2B FinTech means having non-bank providers involved in the process of facilitating these exchanges. This is a welcome change in the B2B transaction landscape, because, with the globalization of markets, direct exchanges of currency become complicated in terms of laws and regulations.

Supply Chains

How does financial technology affect a business's supply chain? It stands a chance to make things easier both for suppliers to a business and their buyers. Both parties benefit from the streamlined process, whereby neither has to concern themselves with carrying out the payments because of its handled by a third party automatically. Furthermore, these transactions can often be done 100 percent electronically, slashing paper waste and reducing the costs associated with these. Not only that but having a third party is particularly helpful with establishing trust among companies because there is an objective participant in overseeing the veracity of the transactions made.

A Weakness

There is a problem in FinTech solutions when dealing with reliable payment types even though the commerce networks that already exist have been developed in order to cater to the needs coming from the B2B crowd. Often times this can be seen when a buyer is looking for a product that they would like to purchase. If you have purchased anything on Amazon, then you know that the prices are going to be different from one seller to another. This happens because of the regulations the seller has to abide by and the volume that they have to offer to their customers.

All of this happens before the client has even completed their purchase. When somewhere around fifty percent of B2B transactions have to be rescheduled or need attention in various other ways, these things have to be done manually. Because of the cost of the resources that are used in order to fix these transactions, many end up being corrected wrong.

Sometimes this is caused because of the data that the merchant has received in the transaction. You will see it happen more when it comes to retailers that use third parties to sell their product. The issues become worse if a product is shipped where FinTech is not available or not in the same language that the merchant speaks.

Since financial institutions have not been forced to keep up with the times, their models tend to fall apart, and their customer service falls between the cracks.

The B2B platforms that are current are fronts for banks when the payment comes into play. Many variables have to be thought of for the B2B scenarios so that they can become traditional models and remain as a customer's go to option. However, because of FinTech, these transaction types could cease to exist if FinTech is adopted throughout the world.

A Dynamic Future

With FinTech, more payment solutions have been created for B2B transactions. These solutions are constantly updating and changing as FinTech upgrades and modifications. Any payment method that stays the same is going to become disconnected from financial services because they are not keeping up with the times. The purpose of these solutions is to allow for proper data management as well as the appropriate security that is needed for every customer. It will allow a supplier and their merchants to have a better grasp on their ever evolving relationship.

A system is more close looped and offers more of a connection when it uses dynamic payments.

FinTech is meant to allow suppliers to discount their products or finance it by just a push of a button. Smart contracts are going to play a role in this system as well to ensure that the merchant is getting the services that are agreed upon by the supplier. If the services or product is not delivered as promised, then the supplier will not receive their payment until it is.

Chapter 6

FinTech and Investing

Fintech is bringing significant changes to the investment industry. The implications are huge—with a globalized market at anyone's fingertips, trading is no longer limited to Wall Street.

Search Terms (Data Analysis)

One aspect that has always been limiting to investors who aren't associated with big firms is that they did not have the same tools that allowed for data collecting on investments. Big banks and companies are able to funnel time and resources into developing advanced analytic programs that allow for close monitoring of the markets. Small-time investors just don't have analytical tools, with the same magnitude, at their disposal—until now. Now, financial data analysis can be crowdsourced and shared with small time investors, which is leveling the playing field for those involved.

A great thing that has come from FinTech is that it follows the news in real time and the trades that need to be made are done without any human intervention. The information that is put into the system is more accurate so that current events and how they are going to affect trading can be rated on a sliding market scale. This information allows investors to see if a trade is going to harm their investments, or help them. It will also tell them how to help their investments so that they can make an informed decision if that trade is right for them.

Social media can be "mined" for data that is valuable, but the information is going to need to be up to date as possible. Not only that, but groups, concepts, and even individuals that are important have to be identified. Companies and countries are going to be analyzed as well. Then, they are going to be linked to the associated sentiments in whether they be positive or negative. From there, the results are going to be compiled, and the data that is useful as to what the public cares about on particular news and trades is going to be extracted and used to better trades.

The analysis of data needs to focus on how many times an event is mentioned on social media as well as be able to determine if that source is credible along with the sentiment that is applied to it. Like most things, though, this is easier said than done. Someone who has an excellent knowledge of the way that sentiments are expressed through a variety of platforms, as well as the understanding of how the sentiments are going to affect the markets, is going to be required in order to analyze the data that is collected.

When data is mined from numerous applications, it is done for several reasons. One is to help improve workflow in the financial sector. Sentiments are not going to affect the price of stocks, but, it is important to understand this market in two different ways. For one, it can be used as an alert to any options that shift rapidly based on a particular market or trade that is currently in question. Secondly, it will provide an easy way for ideas to be crowdsourced for up and coming companies or topics. Any trading that is done based on the news will still have a market in Europe because traders do not have the proper mix of ability and need to practice on it reliably. However, the potential for this trading type will continue to move up is still looking promising. But, some risks are still involved because there are always going to be risks when it comes to market trading. Companies that work with FinTech should make sure that they have the proper security and reliability in order to keep their market shares while this concept becomes part of the main trading strategies.

Regulated Crowdfunding

It doesn't stop at cash investments; there are firms out there facilitating real estate investments these days as well.

Crowdfunding is the practice of getting the funding needed for a project by raising money from a large number of people only paying small amounts. This is done mostly through the internet. With regulated crowdfunding, it is important to understand how all participants work together. This eco-system can only be effective and efficient if the infrastructure is fully integrated. Regulated Crowdfunding Eco-System (RCES) works within a highly regulated environment that is solely determined based on the country or province provided.

Local governments mandate the securities commissions by implementing laws and provide regulations that are to be monitored as well as providing an oversight at which point in time they are going to intervene and impose the necessary penalties and fines. Basically, it is the local government's responsibility to protect investors so that the marketplace is straightforward with only qualified companies participating.

The two types of investors that are going to be found in a regulated crowdfunding are the accredited investors and the non-accredited investors.

Accredited investors are the ones whom the securities commission determines to be high net worth investors who will not catastrophically impact the financial integrity of the company that is seeking funds.

Non-accredited investors are going to make up the rest of the population. These investors typically do not meet the requirements for being labeled an accredited investor but have been demanding access to the early stage investments.

The regulated crowdfunding portals are meant to bring both companies and investors together in a secure online portal. The portal is going to provide a broad range of investment opportunities that are open to both accredited and non-accredited investors alike. The portals are going to vary on how many investment types there are as well as vertical industry sectors.

News Trading

News trading is what will primarily drive the currency market. The market is highly driven by the impact that news carries and to take advantage of the way that the news will affect the market, it is of vital importance to understand how certain news events are going to affect currency in the market. There are three things that all high impact news events bring.

Previous or past: there are times when the market is going to look at the current forecast versus what the previous release was in order to gauge where the improvement is. This will also help in case there is a modification from the past release that could end up causing a surprise on the market.

Forecast or Consensus is when the figure is derived from a survey that is done by news agencies. The forecast number represents market expectations and what the release is going to be. Actual release figure is the when the news actually releases from its official sources.

News trading with FinTech is continuing to show an upward trend. With FinTech news trading, you will find that three major players determine what effect the news has on FinTech. The Dow Jones, Reuters, and Bloomberg are the major news agencies that have the biggest impact on FinTech.

After the major players, you will find that other markets and services will provide information regarding any regulations. Lastly, if you have been on social media, then you know how quickly it reacts to any news. This is going to provide a quick response that will usually be more emotional than factual.

Chapter 7

Fintech and Online Banking

Automation

FinTech has made brilliant strides by allowing banks to automate their processes to be more efficient through the adaptation and improvements that are made in the short term as well as the long term. This is done through the application of a variety of techniques that include the correlation of relevant statistical relationships and how they exist between various data points. You may not understand every detail of a transaction, but you are going to want to understand the general correlations between any data that is similar to the different transactions that happen. This will make it easier to reference later when they are required to again.

Validation is also important since data values will be accounted for in a vacuum and will not be valid. Automated processes need to understand what constraints are naturally applied to the data in question, and then map them out beforehand for faster results. This will make it easier to point out the areas that require further investigation by human components of the broader system.

In addition, the success rate for the validation is going to be determined by the rate of positive feedback that a user leaves the system. This will then be automatically analyzed, and the message will be determined and acted upon accordingly. The rate of positive feedback will also be measured in order to determine, for a while, just how accurate the system is when it comes to automating portions of the process in the right way.

Cash Flow Forecasting

In order to maintain their edge against any new competitors in the online space, banks need to focus on services that they, and their data, can reliably provide. One FinTech related solution that many are currently exploring is what is known as a cash flow forecast generation. This estimate is generated by algorithms that study a customer's history of transactions and then determine the future performance based on the information that it finds. The forecast is then provided as part of the client's profile as a visible proof of additional value.

In order to accurately generate cash flow projections, smart companies will utilize what are known as transactions clusters. Every group is uniquely modeled and then combined with other clusters to determine likely outcomes. Cluster parameters include things like transaction type, geolocation, category, whether a transaction is outgoing or incoming, and the related counterparts. Additionally, groups that are based on time can be arranged on how dissimilar they are to one another; though there are typically other connections that make more sense.

When it comes to small or medium enterprises, it is important for banks to provide predictive analytics that is both adequate and accurate. This will allow them to make more well-informed decisions while also giving them a more concrete view of their dependencies, strengths, and weaknesses. It also makes it easier for them to predict the demand for potentially profitable niche products. They will also be able to provide hazardous supply chain decisions based on currency trends while still remaining on top of their cash flow.

In these cases, it is important that banks strive to keep track of macroeconomic data by allowing users to opt into services that will track customer, vendor, location, sector, employee, and revenue data.
This initial data sample is going to provide the basis for more personalized content moving forward.

Additionally, system data, as well as data from any accountants or accounting software, should be used to help improve the accuracy of various algorithms; this will also improve the accuracy of any outcome scenarios.

If the customer is connected directly to any other banks, that information should also be consulted to ensure that the full picture is being seen. Truth be told, FinTech solutions that provide these types of predictive algorithms are already creating the kind of strong business models that the banks are looking for. Treasury as a service is a byproduct of this trend. The process involves using algorithms to put the data banks have access to, to work. This does not mean that it is without potential risk for any early investors, however. It has yet to be proven that these statistical summaries will return the types of reliable results that are required over the long term. Additionally, when pushed to the fullest limits, it has yet to be seen what the average customer thinks about their data being so vividly displayed.

Chapter 8

A Peek into the Future

The progress that FinTech has made in recent years is remarkable, but it is nothing compared to what is to come. There is much speculation when it comes to the existence of the current financial institutions along with their long term health. With there being a primary reliance on data, it will most likely be one of the major determining factors, and ultimately the winning factor. It has yet to be determined if the winner is going to be a newcomer who has learned that less is more or one of the incumbents that have access to greater amounts of data.

Future Scenarios

It is estimated that by the year 2020, over a million transactions will have taken place online at any given minute. This trend is going to continue to move forward as technology continues to take over our lives. Even though many transactions will occur online, cash is still going to be the primary way many smaller transactions take place. Physical money will probably decrease over time as more of our banking and purchases are done online. With more governments becoming aware of savings that are non-cash solutions, it can end up costing about eighty percent less than savings that are based around a physical currency.

With the information that has been collected, global e-commerce is going to reach about three billion dollars by the year 2018, with mobile payment markets reaching 1.5 billion dollars within the same timeframe. This will most likely coincide with global financing which may be three times greater than the world GDP.

In the past few years, crowdfunding on a worldwide basis has grown at a steady rate. From the years 2013 to 2014, there has been a 167 percent explosion, bringing in around ten billion dollars to the market. Individuals investing in the P2P markets will probably double by the year 2020.

FinTech's Future

It is undoubted that FinTech is going to play a part in the future of the financial institutions that are established, but it is unclear as to what kind of role it will play as of now. It could end up destroying some of the financial institutes that people know while helping others to come into the future and gain more customers. It is also going to help shape them based on several different areas that are connected and are going to continue to evolve into the future. These areas are cryptocurrencies and the technology that is needed to run them along with the data collected and regulations that are going to be followed. But, it is important to remember that technology and the way that they react to the financial world are all going to be related to the customer experience and how well it is. Some signs show that these factors will influence the future of FinTech as a whole, but, the field is still evolving and coming into its own, so it is hard to tell exactly what the results will be as of this moment.

Customer experience: the way that a customer feels, and the experience that they receive is the main key to a market that is going to be fast, efficient, and as simple as possible for their customers. It is going to be hard to tell the difference between the businesses that target other businesses and the ones that target their peers. The experience for the customer is going to continue to improve in order to provide a better service to the client. Financial experts are coming together and combining their strength to provide the ultimate customer experience. This is going to end up changing the usage habits in the long run.

The connection between finances and technology: as the future bares down, the way that the financial sector and even the technology that they use is going to have to be improved in the way that it interacts. These two aspects will need to collaborate and break down any traditional business lines because these lines are steadily becoming blurred thanks to technology.

Data: financial institutes hold a massive amount of data that is going to need to be properly utilized within the FinTech framework. The tools that are available for analyzing this data are becoming easier to be accessed which is driving the price down and making them relatively cheap. Just because they are cheap does not mean that they are not effective. It only means that more companies are able to get their hands on these tools in order to analyze their data so that they can take advantage of it. The insights that they gain from this data is going to help change the things that FinTech promises to come in the future. The institutes that do not take advantage of their data while they are going to end up finding themselves at a disadvantage later on down the road.

Cryptocurrencies: are slowly becoming bigger and will eventually play a more significant role in the future. Blockchain is going to be able to do more in an immediate fashion than it currently can. In turn, this will help to change how trading works and how settlements can be handled in the future. Smart contracts are most likely going to be issued for payments that are both digital and physical so that the process is the same as well as less cumbersome. Payments are going to be expected to be paid out as well as services rendered correctly in order to make sure that the contract remains valid. Blockchain can end up changing the financial sector as a whole in the future because of the endless possibilities that will exist.

Regulations: how FinTech impacts the financial future is going to depend on how the financial sector adapts and eventually evolves to handle FinTech and its various needs. Regulators will need to verify that the field is clear for all those who are involved so that various services are able to work together. This can end up breaking down the walls that have been built up due to competition over the years allowing companies that used to compete against each other to work together to not only make more of a profit but to offer a better customer experience.

FinTech has already become a major part of how banks carry out their practices, and, it is going to continue to change as the need for FinTech increases. Any changes that are made with FinTech will cause the financial sector to be shaken to its core thus causing new regulations to be put into place.

Other Publications

Other books, by Jeff Reed, on Amazon:

- ***Smart Contracts: The Essential Guide to Using Blockchain Smart Contracts for Cryptocurrency Exchange***
-
   Available in Kindle, audiobook, and paperback form.

- ***Blockchain: The Essential Guide to Understanding the Blockchain Revolution***

   Available in Kindle, audiobook and paperback form.

- ***Investing in Ethereum: The Essential Guide to Profiting from Cryptocurrencies***

   Available in Kindle, audiobook and paperback form.

Check out Jeff Reed's other books on Amazon:

http://bit.ly/JeffReedBooks

www.ingramcontent.com/pod-product-compliance
Lightning Source LLC
Chambersburg PA
CBHW060411190526
45169CB00002B/845